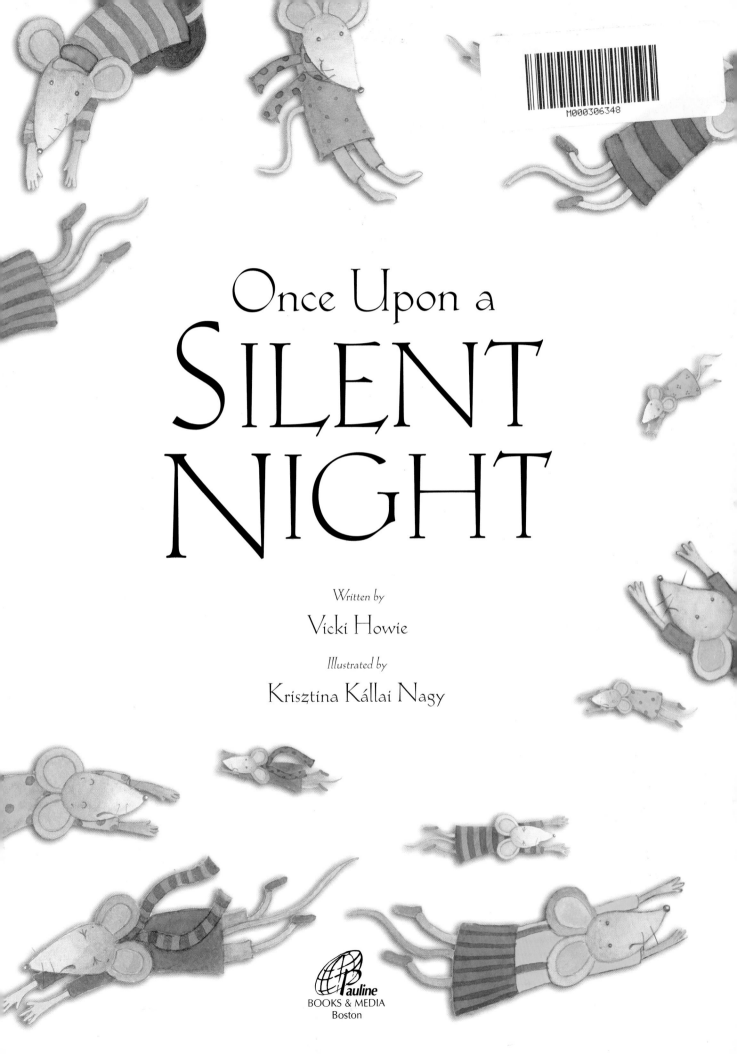

Once Upon a
SILENT
NIGHT

Written by

Vicki Howie

Illustrated by

Krisztina Kállai Nagy

Pauline
BOOKS & MEDIA
Boston

$\mathcal{L}$Long ago,
inside a dusty hole,
hidden in St. Nicholas Catholic Church,
in the heart of the village of Oberndorf,
by a river that rushed helter-skelter
through a land of music and mountains and snow
called Austria,
there lived a large family of mice.

The church mice behaved very badly.

Whenever the church was quiet, they made an absolute mess!

They chased each other up and down the pulpit. They swung on the bell ropes and frayed the ends.

Worst of all, they nibbled here and nibbled there until there were holes in baseboards, kneelers, and choir robes. They nibbled EVERYWHERE!

But whenever Franz Gruber, the organist and
choir director, played his rousing music on the church
organ, the mice went scampering back to their mouse
hole, shaking with fright. Organ music sounds like
thunder to a tiny mouse.

One winter's afternoon, the mice watched as Franz and kind Father Josef Mohr put out the hymn books.

"Are you pleased with the choir, Franz?" asked Father Josef.

"Yes," he replied. "The music is difficult, but the children sing their parts magnificently!"

"I can't wait to hear them tonight at our Christmas Eve Mass!" exclaimed Father Josef. "Their joyful singing is always one of the highlights of Christmas."

The mice looked at one another and squealed in horror.
It was Christmas Eve! Look—there was the Christmas
tree! There was the manger!

Soon Franz would shake the rafters with his
thunderous chords. That organ gave them such a fright.
Let all mice pray for a silent night!

There was no time to lose. The mice could already hear
the choir children outside the church. They were laughing
and singing before their last music practice.

What could the poor church mice do? Mice can only
scamper and nibble and scurry and chew, unless . . .
unless they nibbled a hole in the organ bellows.
That would silence the music!

Nose to tail, the mice raced toward the bothersome organ. Some ran all over the keys. Others found their way to the bellows.

"Look, Franz! Mice!" cried Father Josef.

"Oh, no! Not those little rascals again!" groaned Franz. "Just wait until I catch them!"

The mice began to nibble furiously. They had to make a hole in the leather bellows before the two men reached them! *Nibble, nibble.* They pricked up their ears. Footsteps were coming close. *Nibble, nibble.* They saw two large hands. Surely they would be caught! *Nibble, nibble, puncture ... TEAR!*

Hooray! A hole at last!
With that they ran for their lives and hid.

"Take your places quickly, please, children!" said Franz, unaware of the hole the mice had made. The choir stood in line and waited for Franz to play their introductory music.

But what was this? The organ muttered and spluttered. It gave a cough and a wheeze. Then, silence.

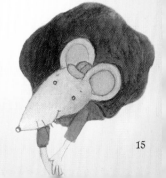

"What shall we do if the organ's broken?" asked a choirboy, almost in tears. "We can't sing our parts without the organ."

"I'm so sorry!" sighed Father Josef. "I know how hard you've all worked. I don't know why the organ won't play, but remember, it's still Christmas Eve. Let's sing a song together to cheer ourselves up."

Father Josef strummed a few chords on his old guitar. It made such a charming sound that the mice crept a little closer.

"Father Josef, why don't you write us a song for Mass tonight?" asked a choirgirl. "You could accompany us on your guitar!"

But Father Josef only shook his head.

"This guitar is too quiet and simple for a celebration as important as Christmas," he said. "No, we will just have to do without your beautiful singing."

The mice watched Franz Gruber leave and the disappointed children trudge back home. This time, they heard no laughing and singing outside the church.

The church was quiet again, but none of the mice wanted
to play. They wished they had not spoiled everyone's
Christmas!

  With heavy hearts, they peeked at the parish
nativity scene. There was Mary, the young mother,
and Saint Joseph, gazing at baby Jesus as he slept
peacefully in the animals' manger. There were
the heavenly angels playing their trumpets
and singing, "Alleluia! Christ the Savior
is born!" There were the shepherds
beaming with love as they knelt
and trembled before the
Son of God.

20

A sound of crinkling paper made the mice look up. A few steps away, Father Josef was unrolling a scroll. On it was a poem he had written two years before.

"*Stille Nacht, Heilige Nacht . . .*"

The mice kept still and listened carefully.
It sounded like the words of a lullaby for baby Jesus.

"I wonder . . . maybe the choirgirl had a point . . ."
muttered Father Josef.

With a nod of his head, he wrapped his cloak around
himself and set out for Franz Gruber's home in the nearby
village of Arnsdorf.

Franz and his family were surprised to have a visitor so late on Christmas Eve. Father Josef explained why he had come.

"Franz," he said, "I need your help. I have a Christmas poem that I wrote a couple of years ago. Could you compose a simple tune for it that I could play on my guitar? We could sing it at Mass tonight, and the choir could join in at the chorus."

"I'll see what I can do," said Franz. "Please, join us for supper, and I'll get to work."

A few hours later the church bell invited the villagers to Midnight Mass.

Clang

Clang

Every row was crammed with families, all expecting to hear the usual magnificent organ music. Instead, they watched Father Josef pick up his guitar.

The church mice hung their heads as Father Josef explained that *something* had gone wrong with the organ that afternoon.

"I didn't know what to do," he said. "The choir thought I should play my guitar, but I did not think it was fancy enough for Christmas. Then as I looked at our nativity scene, I remembered that Jesus, the Son of God, was born in a humble stable. He is happy with simple things, given with love. So Franz and I have written a simple carol. It's called 'Silent Night' and it is our gift to Jesus—and to you."

Father Josef strummed the opening chords, and he and
Franz began to sing:

Silent Night, Holy Night,
All is calm, all is bright,
Round yon Virgin Mother and Child,
Holy Infant so tender and mild,
Sleep in heavenly peace.

"Sleep in heavenly peace!" sang the happy boys and
girls in the choir.

The congregation was so delighted with the new carol, they did not even notice a large family of mice, sleeping peacefully under the Christmas tree.

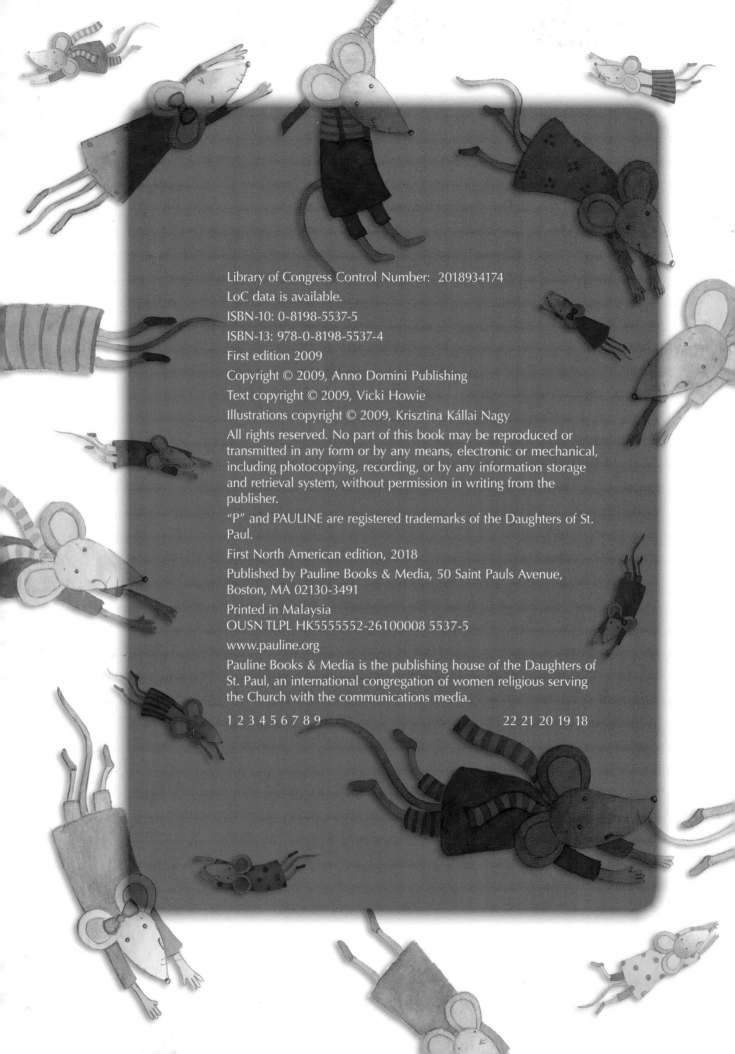

Library of Congress Control Number: 2018934174

LoC data is available.

ISBN-10: 0-8198-5537-5

ISBN-13: 978-0-8198-5537-4

First edition 2009

Copyright © 2009, Anno Domini Publishing

Text copyright © 2009, Vicki Howie

Illustrations copyright © 2009, Krisztina Kállai Nagy

First North American edition, 2018

Published by Pauline Books & Media, 50 Saint Pauls Avenue, Boston, MA 02130-3491

Printed in Malaysia

OUSN TLPL HK5555552-26100008 5537-5

www.pauline.org

Pauline Books & Media is the publishing house of the Daughters of St. Paul, an international congregation of women religious serving the Church with the communications media.

1 2 3 4 5 6 7 8 9   22 21 20 19 18